A Stranger's Journey

By

David W. Thompson

PRESS

Copyright © 2007, 2008 by David W. Thompson

A Stranger's Journey
by David W. Thompson

Printed in the United States of America

ISBN 978-1-60477-471-9

www.xulonpress.com

Table of Contents

Acknowledgements
ix
Best Use
xi
Introduction
xiii
Honor Thy Father and Mother
15
Why is Saying "I am Sorry" so Hard?
17
But I Don't Want to Forgive
19
Sometimes Life Stinks
21
A Life of Indulgence
23
But I'm a Good Christian
25
What is My Soul Worth?
27

Is Being Transparent a Good Thing?
29
Selfish Ambition
31
"If I Only Had …" Living With Regrets
33
"Quiet! Be Still!"
35
They Got What They Deserved
37
It Does Not Feel Light to Me"
39
Betrayal
41
Where Did Everyone Go?
43
It is Called Life
45
Shouldn't Life be Easier Now?
47
Humble Trouble
49
Who Are You Doing it For?
51
For the Cause
53
Membership vs. Relationship
55
Don't Look at Me!
57
Parenting on the Side
59

Bad Company

61

Friendship

63

Do Good

65

Damaged Goods

67

I Lost a Friend Today

69

Remembrance

71

Wordship or Worship

73

Holy Water?

75

Time versus Opportunity

77

The Passion

79

First Impressions

81

Work to Do

83

How Long?

85

More Juice, Please

87

Do it Right the First Time

89

Worry? Who Me?

91

I Expect Service
93
I Want More
95
Give or Take
97
Child Abuse
99
What Do You Think About?
101
Reconciliation to God
103
Reconciled to Self
105
People to People Reconciliation
107
The Spring of Life
109
A Personal Confession
111
Where is Your Quiet Place?
113
The Perfect Child
115
The Color of the Day
117

Acknowledgements

⁓⁓⁓

First and foremost I wish to thank my Lord and Savior, Jesus Christ. He is the reason I am here. He is my guide in this journey.

Also, I wish to thank my wife and faithful companion, Peggy. She encouraged me to write and never lost faith in me. Her tears and laughter let me know my efforts were not in vain.

To the men of my Saturday morning Bible study, I give my thanks and promise my friendship. Thanks for being my sounding board. Your encouragement and suggestions kept me going.

To Kathy, Linda, and Brenda, who took the time to review my work and correct the many grammatical mistakes.

Best Use

This book was written for my Saturday morning men's Bible study and fellowship. Each lesson is designed to stimulate discussion about the scripture verses and their applications in our daily lives.

It is best used when the lesson is studied ahead of time so that participants have time to research their past and present lives in the light of God's word. The study is not about right answers or even being in agreement with the application. It is designed to stretch your thinking and to open up honest dialog with other believers.

If you use the study in this fashion, you will have a full year of thought-provoking fellowship with God and friends. It took a year to write. Why not take a year to enjoy it with others?

Introduction

⸻

"Dear friends, I urge you, as aliens and
strangers in the world, to abstain from sinful
desires, which war against your soul."

1 Peter 2:11 NIV

Have you ever noticed that as we attempt to walk
in a way that honors and pleases God, we not
only look strange or different to the world but also to
ourselves? When we are walking His walk, we are
aliens and strangers to this world. We should not be
surprised when people shake their heads in dismay
or wonder. In fact, we will often surprise ourselves
when we walk spiritually in spite of human nature.

I constantly amaze myself with the good that I
do when I would much prefer to do just the opposite.
For me the battle is allowing God to direct my path
rather than relying on myself or the world to deter-
mine my course. It has always been easier to trust in
what I can see or in what I think I know. Some might

say and rightly so, "You need to increase in faith." The truth is we all could stand to grow in our faith.

This Bible study is for me a faith walk. I am not a professional writer. I am only a man who wants to please God in spite of my sinful nature. When you are a child of God, this earthly life can be a great struggle. You get to experience the trials and the victories of everyday living. Some are great and some are small but almost everyone leaves us with choices and questions.

I pray you will enjoy and learn from my thoughts and questions, as I, a stranger, pass through this very strange land called life.

David W. Thompson
Men's Bible Study Minister

Honor Thy Father and Mother

———— ❦ ————

"Honor your father and mother" – which is the first commandment with a promise – 'that it may go well with you and that you may enjoy long life on the earth.'"

Ephesians 6:2-3 NIV

In a world of tell it like it is and under the banner of being completely honest, more and more people are forgetting the importance of honoring our parents. I say "our" because I can be and have been just as guilty as the next person. I have not found any Scripture that tells me that the children are to raise up the parents. However, how many times do we see the children calling all the shots for the parents? While it is true we are all brothers and sisters in Christ, I have not found any reference to children having the responsibility of correcting a parent's actions or life-style. If we know someone caught in a sin we are to go to them in love and show them their fault. But, we need to be careful, because too many times we react to what we perceive as an injustice to us and it is not an actual sin on their part.

Do children have the ability or authority to change a lifetime of acquired personality traits of their parents? I only see heartache in the attempt. Shouldn't we love and honor our parents for whom God has made them? Life is not fair and God has never promised it to be that way. One child might take more attention than another, due to health or other issues. Another child may think he or she has been swept aside and feels like the other is more favored. And one child may be more favored. Take the story of Joseph, for example. Does favoritism mean a lack of love? A more interesting question would be, "Does a lack of love give someone the right to dishonor a parent?"

The truth is we may not like what our parents are or how they parent, but we are still called to honor. To do otherwise puts us squarely opposite of God's command and that is by definition "SIN". If you have had an issue with this type of behavior, I suggest that you follow the words of Jesus Christ, "Go and sin no more".

Why is Saying "I am Sorry" so Hard?

⸺⸻

"Therefore, if you are offering your gift at the altar and there remember that your brother has something against you; leave your gift there in front of the altar. First go and be reconciled to your brother; then come and offer your gift." Matthew 5:23-24 NIV

What a question! All of us have struggled with this issue. To say otherwise would certainly be untrue and would lead us to bigger issues. The Bible teaches us to be reconciled with our brothers and sisters in Christ. It is good for us. It is good for them. Most importantly, it is good for the church as a whole. God wants His church to be healthy. If you or someone else has a problem with admitting their trespasses against another and apologies are not given and received, we the church will never be completely healthy.

Knowing the importance of forgiveness should be obvious to the Christian. Without God's forgiveness we have no hope for eternity. If we know that our sins against God need to be forgiven, what would make us believe that our sins against others are not worthy of an apology?

With this being said, and because of the knowledge we have been given, why do we still refuse at times to seek forgiveness? It happens in the church, in the home, with friends, at work and anywhere else where more than one person exists. The list of "whys" is long. A few of the more obvious reasons are pride, anger, fear of rejection and fear of consequence. All of our reasons do nothing but keep us in bondage. God's plan keeps us free. If we can learn to apologize and really mean it, which means we should not repeat it, our hearts and spirits will be free from excessive burden. Knowing that you have hurt someone else and never making amends will only weigh you down.

Saying "I am sorry" and truly meaning it will remove the emotional bondage in which you have placed yourself. The forgiveness part is on the other party, and that is a lesson for another day.

"But I Don't Want to Forgive"

—⚬⚬⚬—

"For if you forgive men when they sin against you, your heavenly Father will also forgive you. But if you do not forgive men their sins, your Father will not forgive your sins." Matthew 6: 14-15 NIV

When the Bible gives us a warning it is in our best interest to heed it. Human nature is not prone to forgive. The new nature we have in Christ is in constant war with the fleshly nature when it comes to forgiveness. How many times have we heard someone say, "I can never forgive that person for what they have done!" We live in a fallen world that brings so much pain and heartache to people, one can understand why it becomes hard to forgive.

The real issue for the Christian is to rise above the ordinary and become extraordinary in this area. We speak volumes to the world when we can show true forgiveness to another. In forgiving, we set ourselves apart from the world and show a quality that draws men to a forgiving Savior. If we who represent Christ show forgiveness, the lost have a living example of God's mercy.

The other side of the issue is that when a Christian refuses to show forgiveness, he or she is showing the world an untrue picture of God. Why would a lost person want to become a Christian if he sees God's children as bitter and unforgiving people? For us to refuse to forgive puts us squarely at odds with our Master.

The refusal to forgive has no benefit for anyone. The one who does not receive it is harmed and the one who does not give it carries it with him where ever he goes. Unforgiveness will become the norm in a person's life unless he learns to do otherwise.

It never gets less. It only adds to the load. It will make one's life miserable and unproductive for the kingdom of God.

If you are having trouble forgiving others, start with the small things first. God will help you take the small steps and will ultimately get you to where you can handle the big ones also. But, by all means start. You do not want to be out of God's will. It is just not worth it.

Sometimes Life Stinks

⸺◈⸺

"But the Lord provided a great fish to swallow Jonah, and Jonah was inside the fish three days and three nights." Jonah 1:17

All of us will have times when life is difficult. In fact, there will be times when it just stinks. Try to imagine yourself in Jonah's situation. First, God speaks to him and gives him an assignment that he believes will not make him very popular with the people of Nineveh. Next, he tries to run away from his duty, which is not very smart. He takes passage on a ship, endangers the lives of the others on the ship, and is eventually tossed overboard. Finally, he is swallowed by a great fish. This, of course, is not the whole story, but it certainly helps make a point. Life is not always good.

Three days in the belly of a fish does not sound like a vacation cruise. What else might be in the fish's belly? (Decaying fish, sea weed and other sea creatures, for sure) I can only imagine the smell and discomfort. After all this, what kind of hope would you have?

Here is something for you to think about. If God had not sent the fish, Jonah would have probably drowned. The fish was not his punishment. It was his protection sent by God. Sometimes God will send hard times our way. It may be the result of our rebellion to what God wants us to do, or it may be there to serve as a protection for us. God desires only the best for us, but sometimes the best is found after we pass through the belly of adversity. I can not tell you how many times I have seen God take something that appeared to be bad or even hopeless, only to reveal a great and wonderful purpose years later.

Has life been tough? You need to ask why? Maybe it is time to see if you have been running from God, or if He is just offering you protection in a way that you do not fully understand. Take time today to talk to Him, because He really does care.

A Life of Indulgence

—∞∞∞—

"When he heard this, he became very sad,
because he was a man of great wealth. Jesus
looked at him and said, 'How hard it is for the
rich to enter the kingdom of God!'"

Luke 18:23-24.

You probably know the story; a rich and powerful
man asked Jesus how he could inherit eternal
life. When questioned about his obedience to the
laws of God, he claimed to be without fault, but in
the end, he left unhappy.

Since, the Scripture refers to him as being a ruler;
one can make an argument that he was born into a
family of power and wealth. He would have been
educated and trained by the finest teachers available.
The prestige of his family in some ways allowed him
to be indulged.

Indulgence can lead to dependence. When life
is easy, we expect it to stay easy. Indulgence brings
expectations which can be unrealistic. If we over

indulge our children, they may be viewed by others as spoiled or pampered, and that may be the case. God is capable of indulging His children, but He knows that there must be a balance. He also knows that an easy life can cause us to be complacent in our spiritual walk.

How many times have we watched news stories of the very rich who have fallen from grace in the world's view? They no longer have society's approval or the indulgences that it can bring. They lose hope and fall into ruin. For many, life is not worth living and they choose suicide.

Our rich ruler lost heart when Jesus asked him to give up his wealth and indulgences to follow Him. Are we any different? When we are asked to give sacrificially, do we follow through? When we are asked to give of our time, do we put pleasures aside? Do we grumble when life turns from easy to hard because we have become complacent?

The truth is that the ruler could have had treasures beyond his wildest dreams had he been willing to walk away from his life of indulgence.

But I'm a Good Christian

—❦—

"As Jesus started on his way, a man ran up to him and fell on his knees before him. 'Good teacher,' he asked, 'what must I do to inherit eternal life?' 'Why do you call me good?' Jesus answered. 'No one is good- except God alone.'" Mark 10:17-18 NIV

Recently, I was made aware of a meeting between a contractor and a local businessman. The contractor was bidding on a construction job and wanted it badly. One reason he gave to consider giving him the job was that, "I am a good Christian businessman." Have you ever met this kind of person? Does being a Christian give us a special privilege in the business world?

I grew up under the understanding that as a Christian, I am a sinner saved by God's amazing grace. The term "sinner" does not sound like a good thing to me. For years I have dealt with people who want to use their Christianity as leverage in the business world. In other words, they want you to do them a favor because they profess to be a follower of Christ. A good friend of mine who is a very successful businessman told me once that when a customer or a prospective customer comes in, he watches them with at least one eye, but when they start talking about how good a Christian they are, he has both eyes open.

It would seem to me that if I have to tell someone how good of a Christian I am, I have already missed the target. My actions need to speak louder than my words. My conduct and reputation should be able to speak for me. Isn't it a shame that too many times what we claim to be is not reflected in the actions that people see?

Now, where in the world do some people get the idea that being a Christian should bring special privileges? The Bible talks of persecutions and sufferings for being a Christian but not any earthly privileges. Spiritual privileges, yes. Worldly, no.

Friends, if someone asks you to do something for him or her solely because they are Christian, keep both eyes open as you walk away.

What is My Soul Worth?

—— ⌘ ——

"What good will it be for a man if he gains the whole world, yet forfeits his soul? Or what can a man give in exchange for his soul?" Matthew 16:26.

This verse says a lot more to me than just losing your soul to hell. For me, it speaks about my spiritual integrity. Man is made in the image of God, but many times we are a very poor reflection of our Creator.

In my effort to become a success in the world of business, I find that everyday I must face choices. The world view is doing whatever it takes to get the job done. The real question for me is, "Am I willing to give up Godly principles to achieve worldly results?" I would like to be able to say that I have always made the right choice, but that would not be true. There have been times in my life when presented with a choice between results and principles, I have chosen poorly. When I have made the wrong choice, I have not only let myself down but God also. What I may have gained is not even close to what I have lost.

Some businessmen might say, "Well, there was no real harm to anyone, and you did get the job done with the desired results." No real harm done? I have just taken another step away from being a clear image of my Heavenly Father. I weep at the thought of losing my integrity if even for an instant. There is absolutely no reason to shortcut God's principles.

This world will continue to battle with me until my Lord calls me home. There will be times when I will fail, but there will be times when I, with the aid of the Holy Spirit, will rise above this world and do what is right in the sight of God. I pray that I will continue to grow spiritually and become a better reflection of the One who gives me life.

Everyday there will be choices. How will you choose?

Is Being Transparent a Good Thing?

———— ∞∞∞ ————

"Do nothing out of selfish ambition or vain conceit, but in humility consider others better than yourselves." Philippians 2:3 NIV

Through the years I have met some very interesting characters with some very interesting points of view. An acquaintance of mine once said that she had reached the age where she no longer needed to watch how she spoke to people, that people could accept her just the way she was, and that if they did not like it, that was too bad. I have also talked to other people who felt that they did not need to account for their actions to anyone for the same reason.

Where do people get the idea that what they say or do requires no accountability? Strangely enough, I find this attitude has a strong base in the Christian community. We live in a "tell it like it is" world and to be sure as a Christian, I must tell the Gospel of

Jesus Christ just like it is. However, beyond that, having the appearance of transparency to justify my personal attitudes or beliefs does not work. Honesty and transparency are two different things but are often confused.

Some Christians believe they have been given license to be brutally honest or transparent because they have a gift of prophesy. Have you ever received a rebuke that started out with the words, "Now this is for your own good," only for it to turn out to have no benefit at all? I have heard people say, "I was just being completely honest," trying to justify the hurt they inflicted upon someone else. Through the years with much practice, I have learned to tell people the truth in a non-threatening manner. I have noticed that most people can receive the truth, no matter how hard it may be, if the delivery is proper. Even a rebuke does not have to be bitter if it is done in love. "Speak the truth in love." Ephesians 4:15.

Honesty is the best policy. But we need to be careful to use it to build up, not to tear down.

Selfish Ambition

—— ∞∞∞ ——

"Do nothing out of selfish ambition or vain conceit, but in humility consider others better than yourselves." Philippians 2:3 NIV

Did you ever wonder why decisions always come down to others or self? Every day we are faced with decisions. Decisions will always have an effect on someone or something. Have you ever had to make a decision that would have a good effect on someone but a bad effect on yourself? Or have you ever made a decision that would be good for you but bad for someone else?

Ambition can be a very good thing when it is channeled for God's purpose. It also can bring death and destruction when it is only used for selfish purposes. As God's children we need to be careful to examine the motives behind our decisions.

Several years ago during a critical moment in my life, that small quiet voice spoke to my heart. "It is really not about you or what you want. It is about what I need you to do." My life has never been the same since. Now, more than ever, I take the time to see who or what is going to be affected by the decisions I make.

Please understand that I am not saying that I always make the right decisions. Many of the choices I make suit me more than others. Obviously, I have not achieved the humility that Jesus Christ displayed. Chances are I will never make it that far, but I must try.

If you are like me and have trouble from time to time with selfish ambition in your decision making process, join with me today in making one very important decision. Let's decide today to put self aside and take upon ourselves a Christ-like humility in all our choices so that others are not hurt unnecessarily, and God's purposes are achieved through us.

"If I Only Had ....."
Living with Regrets

‒‒‒⟨ ∽∾∽ ⟩‒‒‒

"Godly sorrow brings repentance that leads to salvation and leaves no regret, but worldly sorrow brings death."

2 Corinthians 7:10 NIV

How many times do we think or say, "if I only had"? If I had only been there. If I had only said this or not said that. If I had only made the right choice. Life is full of "ifs." A better word is regrets.

I have heard people say, "I have no regrets about my life." How can this possibly be? Have we become so hardened to our failures that they just do not matter?

Personally, I think that if we say we have no regrets, we are lying to the world and ourselves. I regret that I have not been the Christian example that God wants me to be. What if I had read my Bible more? What if I had been a better witness to the lost?

What if I had been a better spouse or parent? My list can go on and on. How about yours?

This is just a thought but if a person has no regrets has he ever truly lived? And if I say "I have no regrets," have I come to a point of true repentance? Let's face it; we all have regrets. The real key for us is how well we live with them.

God does not want us to live a life of defeat. God wants us to overcome our regrets and failures. The truth is He wants us to learn from them so that they do not have to be repeated. Simply put, if you do not want to have regrets, do not repeat past failures. Another good way to avoid regrets is to think before you say or do something. A little prayer and planning can go a long way.

Thank God there are some things that we do not regret: our salvation, family and friends. A good way to live is to focus on the "I'm glad I dids" of our lives. I can truly live when I remember the good I did do rather than my failure to do what was good. People who dwell on their regrets will not find happiness or forgiveness.

"Quiet! Be Still!"

⸺ ∞ ⸺

"He got up, rebuked the wind and said to
the waves, 'Quiet! Be still!' Then the wind
died down and it was completely calm."

Mark 4:39 NIV

Isn't it amazing we can read and believe that our
God has authority over the storms of nature, yet
we panic just like Jesus' disciples when spiritual
and personal storms begin to batter us? At this very
moment a category 3 hurricane has hit the gulf coast
of Texas and Louisiana. Our God, by speaking a
word, can stop it immediately. He may choose not
to do so, but that does not change the fact that He
is able. Great storms of nature can devastate entire
regions. Great personal and spiritual storms can
devastate families and churches.

When hurricanes head toward land, people are
given the opportunity to flee from their paths and find
shelter to ride out the storm. God gives us the same
options when life comes crashing down. We can flee

to His side and find safety and shelter in Him. I can not tell you how many times God has rescued me in the midst of personal and spiritual trials. Each and every time, He amazes me with His power and grace.

We are created beings with a special, but not always beneficial, free will. We can choose to panic or we can choose to trust. More times than I like to admit, I panic. The magnitude of the impending storm can be so overwhelming that my ability to reason is gone. I panic. I break and run. I will do things that just defy reason.

Have you ever found yourself in such a panic that you could see no way out? I am so glad that God knows exactly what is going to happen. It is a great joy and comfort for me to know that the God of Heaven is concerned about me. There have been times when during the storms I have heard God's voice, "Quiet! Be still!" Then it becomes calm, and I begin to see the big picture. I see God's plan and purpose. Panic is no longer an option because God has taken control of the situation.

May we all learn to trust more and have faith that God is in control of the lives of His children.

"They Got What They Deserved"

—————

"Finally, all of you, live in harmony with
one another; be sympathetic, love as brothers,
be compassionate and humble."

1 Peter 3:8 NIV

Does anybody live up to this verse? Not to be
critical, but if you are saying, "Yes, that is me",
we need to talk. Have you ever had a disagreement
with a brother or sister of the faith? Have you ever
made the statement, "They got what they deserved"?
Have you ever been so sure you were correct that
you bullied another believer into submission? Have
you turned your back on someone because he failed
morally? If you can say yes to any or all of these
questions, do not despair, you are not alone.

Like many Christians, I have spent most of
my life in church. Saved at a young age trained by
good teachers in the Scriptures, shouldn't I have the
ability to live out this one verse? We may have the

knowledge and the training, but if we are not willing to put them into practice, what good are they.

If you hang around Christians long enough, you will find out that they are not superhuman with an ability to not sin. In fact, you will come to realize that they are just human beings capable of committing any sin that can be imagined. I am not trying to make excuses here. I am just stating a fact. The big difference is we know we are sinners and know where our salvation comes from. Thank you, Jesus!

It is a true puzzlement to me why we oftentimes rejoice when other Christians fall. Where is the love, compassion or sympathy? It has been said that we Christians are an army that shoots our wounded.

If we got what we deserved, we would be burning in hell right now. God demonstrated his love and sympathy and compassion by sending His Son. Jesus showed us humbleness and restored harmony between us and the Father. Should we not desire to be able to do the same? Hard work I know, but what a world we could make!

"It Does Not Feel Light to Me"

———— ᴏᴆᴂᴐ ————

"For our light and momentary troubles are
achieving for us an eternal glory that far out
weighs them all." 2 Corinthians 4:17 NIV

I don't know about you, but some of the troubles
I have dealt with in my life did not feel very
light. How easy it is for me to get on a pity party?
Employment problems, family problems, illnesses,
and the list can go on. How could Paul write such
things? He had been beaten, arrested and persecuted.
He had an affliction that God chose not to heal. He
knew he would ultimately die for his faith. Yet he
could consider these issues light?

If we had been in Paul's position, would we have
been able to make such a statement? The longer God
allows me to live the more I learn. I can now look
back and see past problems that seemed insurmount-
able, but I did survive. I can look at some of my
infirmities, but somehow I still manage, and in some
cases, I have actually overcome them.

I also look forward with great anticipation to the day when God calls me home. What a day that will be!

Am I saying I have reached the level of understanding that Paul had acquired? Absolutely not! I am not even close. I wonder though, how much more crushing it would be without Christ. How do you handle problems without hope? What if we could not take them to God in prayer? Imagine a world where everyone is left to their own devises or solutions. Where would we be without the truth of the Scriptures?

A thought comes to me as I write this devotional. My troubles may not seem light or momentary to me, but to God they are not problems at all. He can carry my load and is willing to do so. But first, I have to lay it down and let Him carry it for me.

No matter what you may be facing today, remember someday all these things will indeed pass away.

Betrayal

———⠀⠀⠀———

"But the hand of him who is going to betray me is with mine on the table."

Luke 22:21 NIV

Have you ever felt the awful pain of betrayal? Chances are you have. Whether the matter is large or small, the pain can be almost unbearable. Those of us who know the story understand that even Jesus Christ, the Son of God, had to face being betrayed. Thus, it should not surprise us then when we must face it in our own lives.

Why does betrayal hurt so much? My thought is because it is usually done by someone who is close to you and you trusted them. Marriages end every day because a spouse yields to temptation and breaks the bonds of trust that are a critical part of the marriage covenant. It may be sexual infidelity. It may be a lack of honesty involving finances or other areas of family life. It can even be a lack of protection for the spouse. It does not stop with marriages. It can happen between parent and child, between siblings, friends, business associates, and even church members.

It can happen in small matters as well as large life-changing situations. It can sometimes cost a person their life. We know that ultimately Judas's betrayal led to Jesus's death on the cross, which was part of a greater plan. It also led to Judas's death by his own hand, because of the grief and despair it brought.

Sometimes the cost may seem small, but is the loss of trust ever to be considered small? All good relation-ships are based on trust. Take a moment to reflect on your life if you could not trust those around you. Now take another moment to reflect on all those who have placed their trust in you. Is betrayal worth it?

I urge you to always consider your actions care-fully. If your action is going to break trust with someone else don't do it. Trust is precious and not easily restored.

Where Did Everyone Go?

⚯

"One of the high priest's servants, a rela-
tive of the man whose ear Peter had cut off,
challenged him, 'Didn't I see you with him in
the olive grove?' Again Peter denied it and at
that moment a rooster began to crow."

John 18 26 & 27. NIV

Have you ever had the feeling that you were
all alone in a very difficult situation? Most of
us can answer a definite yes to this question. When
we hit those hard times, and all our friends seem to
disappear, the pain seems to intensify.

I can not imagine how it must have been for
Jesus. His inner circle, those closest to him-not there
for him. How do you face persecution and ultimately
death without help, especially when you are inno-
cent? Yes, we can say that God was with him, but the
Bible tells us that even God in the end could not look
upon Him because of the sin He bore.

I am not foolish enough to compare my hard times to Christ's sufferings. But, they do give me at least a glimpse of what He went through.

Maybe you have been abandoned by a marriage partner. Or perhaps you have experienced the painful absence of friends and family when times got bad. It is not a pleasant place to be. How do I go on? What do I do next? Who can help me? Where did I go wrong? These are all questions for which we are often unable to find answers for because those we need to help us are no longer available. It can be a deep hole of despair. Sometimes it is more than an individual can bear and he breaks. It may be mentally, physically and even spiritually. The thing is he breaks.

Have you been there? Or maybe you are there right now. My friend, there is hope. Because of the sacrifice on the cross, you are never alone. As a Christian, God sees you through the shed blood of Jesus. He can look upon you even in your sin because it no longer exists to Him. Jesus has paid the price. Your sin debt has been paid in full! So friend, if you think you are alone, think again. Lift up your eyes and cry out to the Lord; you will find comfort. You are not alone.

It is Called Life

"Therefore I tell you, do not worry about your life, what you will eat or drink; or about your body, what you will wear. Is not life more important than food, and the body more important than clothes?" Matthew 6:25 NIV

My wife and I were driving to the restaurant for dinner and she made what I thought was a very astute comment. "The only problem with life is that life gets in the way." What a thought!

As children we make plans to be cowboys or pirates, but life comes along and says, "Sorry that is not going to happen." In our teen years we plan to become rock musicians or professional athletes, but life again says, "You are not in that one percent who can make it." As young adults we plan careers after college. Do you know how many times the average college student changes his major? We get married and we plan for the perfect life. What do we get? I will let you fill in your own blank.

Is it possible we do not understand the true nature of life? Do we expect too much from it? Is what we call life really what God intended for us?

Life is the road we must travel to get to our final destination. Unfortunately, it is not always a super highway with smooth pavement and every bump or curve plainly marked. Life is more like the old logging roads that I traveled as a child hunting wild game in the hills of Missouri with my father. They were winding, muddy and sometimes treacherous.

Let's face it. The life we live out here on earth is not designed to always be easy. We learn from bumps and bruises. We change courses after trial and tragedies. We gain wisdom from failures. Sometimes things happen that just do not make any sense. Unfortunately, we can not run and hide from life. It will always find us.

God has equipped His people to handle life. I am convinced that He not only wants us to handle the twist and turns of life but to enjoy and learn from them. Look at it this way. When things are going good, life is not boring. When things are going bad, life is not boring. If nothing good or bad ever happened, wouldn't life be boring?

My friends, be brave; be courageous; God is in control.

Shouldn't Life be Easier Now?

—⚬⚬⚬—

"For it has been granted to you on behalf
of Christ not only to believe on him, but also
to suffer for him." Philippians 1:29 NIV

There is a popular teaching going around that
says, "If we are Christians and we are living a
life that is pleasing to God, we will not have hard-
ships." If this is true, most of the Christians I know,
including myself, have really missed the mark. If this
teaching has any basis in the Bible, I can not find
it. I feel sorry for the person who buys into such a
philosophy because he will constantly be trying to
second guess God when things get tough.

If life were always good and contained no hard-
ships, don't you think we would become complacent
in our Christianity? Wouldn't we serve more out of
fear of losing favor than out of love? Would we be
serving God or trying to earn blessings?

I do not know what the percentage is, but it
seems to me more lessons are learned from our

struggles than from our blessings. To illustrate what I am saying, think about this. You do not learn to ride a bicycle because someone gave it to you, and you instinctively know how to ride. The bicycle may be a blessing, but you learn to ride through instruction, trial, and error. When I was a young boy and my parents bought me my first bicycle, they did not get one that had training wheels. Learning to ride quickly became an adventure and a hazardous one at that. Ultimately, I learned to ride because I got tired of making the same mistakes and crashing. If I had the attitude that nothing should be hard, I would have given up after the first bandage was applied.

Life is a learning process and most of the time life is not easy. What we learn as a Christian is that although we suffer, we do not suffer alone. God is always there. He never takes a break or takes a nap. God, in His grace, allows hard times so that we can learn and be better prepared to help others when they go through the same thing. God did not spare His own Son from suffering persecution and death, so why would I think I deserve an exemption.

God does not promise life without trouble. He does promise that we do not have to face it alone.

Humble Trouble

———— ⊶⊷ ————

"Be completely humble and gentle: be
patient, bearing with one another in love."
Ephesians 4:2 NIV

Do you know a Christian who fits this verse?
Probably you do. But don't you also know
Christians who are anything but humble? Often the
cause of Christ is hurt by the very people who claim
to be His disciples. Most people are turned off by
arrogant or haughty attitudes in business and personal
relationships. It would only make sense then that an
arrogant Christian is a turn- off for a lost person.

Just to think of this brings back many bad memo-
ries. The high and mighty, the holier-than-thou
Christians cause pain wherever they go. As a rebel-
lious teenager, I used these sorts of people to excuse
my absence from the fellowship. The lost people use
them for excuse also. If you have ever been involved
in a visitation program, you know what I am talking
about. More than once I have had a person tell me

that they know a Christian, and if they have to be like him they do not want any part of it.

In the book of Philippians Chapter 2 we are told in Verse 5, "Your attitude should be the same as that of Christ Jesus." Now, I have never found where Christ showed arrogance in the Scriptures. But, you will find the term humble, humility or servant used.

Before you consider me a finger pointer, let me confess that I have caught myself being anything but humble. I can be arrogant without saying a word. I can think myself better than the next man and prove it by not being willing to humble myself and give a witness to the lost. I can assume that my time is more important than God's. If that isn't a lack of humility I don't know what is. I am a sinner saved by grace- nothing more. My salvation has nothing to do with position, wealth or personal character. Every once in a while, I forget the spiritual state where I began. I am sure I am not alone.

One thing I want us to remember: God has the ability to humble mighty men. With just a word from Him, kings and kingdoms have and will fall.

Who Are You Doing it For?

———— ∞∞∞ ————

"But when you give to the needy, do not let your left hand know what the right hand is doing," Matthew 6:3 NIV

There are many things in life that make us feel good. One thing for the Christian is doing a good deed for someone else. What a pleasure to bless people when they have a need even if it appears to be insignificant. I can guarantee that those who have the need do not consider it that way.

There is something special about helping others and knowing you are making a difference in their lives. There is one concern here that we need to consider. Who are we doing it for? Are we doing it for God, or are we doing it to just feel good about ourselves? If we are doing our good deeds for our Heavenly Father, then a by-product of our action is being able to feel good also. If we do things just to make us feel good, then the Father does not get the glory.

The best good deed we can do is the one that nobody else knows about, only you and the person you help. There are times when even the person being helped does not have to know who it was that cared. Now, God really gets the credit in that case.

The Word tells us that if we publicly do our good deeds, our reward is from the public. Everyone likes to be recognized and appreciated so sometimes it can be hard to keep from talking about what we have done. When we do this, we pat ourselves on the back. I believe if God wants the world to know of my good deeds, He will make them known.

We should be conscious of our motives in doing good deeds. Do we want God's approval or man's? Wouldn't it be awful to stand at the throne of the King and not hear, "Well done thou good and faithful servant."

For the Cause

⬥⬥⬥

"….But as for me and my household, we will serve the Lord." Joshua 24:15 NIV

It seems everyone today fights for some cause. Some work tirelessly for charities. Others fight for political change. Some save babies while others save rain forests. There are those who raise the banner of self and give their all to increase their wealth and power. All these causes may serve to do good and can be of benefit to many. Even the selfish causes can have good results.

But all these things we serve, work, and fight for pale in comparison to the greatest cause of all, the cause of Christ. Whatever we or the world may gain through good works and deeds, through politics and social change, and by means of power and wealth, ultimately, will be laid to waste. The only thing remaining will be the soul standing in judgment before God. What good will all the things we have held to be important be if we have never accepted Jesus Christ as our Lord and Savior?

I am not saying that charities are not important or that protecting the unborn or helpless children are not noble endeavors. Politics has its place as well as social change. Wealth and power are sometimes essential in the stewardship of this world we have been given. I am convinced, though, that all these are by-products, and therefore secondary, to the cause of knowing Christ. The Bible states it like this, "What good will it be for a man if he gains the whole world and yet forfeits his soul? Or what can a man give in exchange for his soul?" Matthew 16:26 NIV.

We can serve many causes, but the greatest is to serve Christ by telling others of His grace, forgiveness and salvation. May we fight the good fight well!

Membership vs. Relationship

"Yet a time is coming and has now come when true worshipers will worship the Father in spirit and truth, for they are the kind of worshipers the Father seeks." John 4:23 NIV

Just because we are members of a local church does not mean we are true worshipers of God. I am constantly amazed at the misguided attitude that says I have my church membership; therefore, I am secure and heaven bound. This is like rappelling down the side of a mountain and saying that because I have a rope in my hand I am safe. What if the other end of the rope is not tied to something solid?

You can have memberships in churches of every denomination known to man yet be falling into the pit of hell. I remember when a certain church in my hometown was having a huge fallout over a political comment made by the pastor from the pulpit. One member went as far as to chastise the church and the pastor in a letter to the editor of the local paper. At the beginning of his letter, he informed the public that he had been a member of the church for over 20 years. This came as quite a surprise to most of the church's congregation since he had not attended a service in 20 years.

Many churches take time to purge their membership roles of those people who have not participated in some fashion with the church for several years. It never fails that some, when contacted about their membership being removed, become insulted and angry. They cling to the membership as if it were the last ticket on the last bus leaving town.

I am not saying that membership is not important. In fact the Bible teaches otherwise. What I am saying is that membership will not get you to Heaven; only the personal relationship that a Christian has with Jesus Christ counts. I am not trying to pass judgment on those who hold their church membership with very high regard. I too value my church membership, but not as my ticket to the Promised Land. I value it because I have developed relationships with my church family.

If you have a church membership, I implore you to use it to develop relationships with other children of God and to come together with them in worshiping Him in spirit and in truth.

Don't look at me!

"For the grace of God that brings salvation has appeared to all men. It teaches us to say 'No' to ungodliness and worldly passions, and to live self-controlled, upright and godly lives in this present age, while we wait for the blessed hope-the glorious appearing of our great God and Savior, Jesus Christ, who gave himself for us to redeem us from all wickedness and to purify for himself a people that are his very own, eager to do what is good."

Titus 2:11-14 NIV.

"Don't look at me. I am not perfect or without sin." How many of us use this excuse? I certainly have. There is plenty of truth in the statement, but to use it as an excuse concerning my behavior just does not work.

We need to be so careful if we call ourselves Christian. When someone compliments me for upright behavior, do I accept the praise for myself? Well, if I can do that, then I better be able to take the heat when rebuke comes for my sinful behavior. My nature likes praise, but it certainly does not like criticism.

I realize that when I am apart from Jesus Christ, I am a sinner on my way to hell. In Christ, I am a sinner saved by His grace. In both situations, I am still a sinner. As a Christian, all praise I receive should be given to Him. All rebuke I receive for my actions is deserved and should be taken to heart so that I can be a better witness for Christ. The Bible says in Proverbs 9:8-9 "Do not rebuke a mocker or he will hate you; rebuke a wise man and he will love you. Instruct a wise man and he will be wiser still; teach a righteous man and he will add to his learning."

So what is my excuse for using this excuse? "Hey, I am a sinner. Don't look at me."

Parenting on the Side

───── ❦ ─────

"If anyone does not provide for his relatives, and especially for his immediate family, he has denied the faith and is worse than an unbeliever."

1 Timothy 5:5 NIV

Has anyone else noticed that parenting has changed drastically in the last three generations? Maybe I am overreacting but it sure seems to me that more and more parents view parenting as a hobby rather than a full-time commitment. If there is truth to this observation, we may find that many of our present social issues come from parenting on the side.

The verse in 1 Timothy is usually tied to financial provision. I believe that it is much broader than that. As a parent, I know that God wants me to provide for my family (especially children) with more than just money. He desires that I train them to be good citizens spiritually, socially and financially. Somewhere along the way, our personal lives have become separated from our parental duties. I watch people with their children and how they interact, and it appears that in many cases, the children call the shots. I have seen four-year-old children decide where the family will eat, shop, vacation and even go to church. It would appear that roles have somehow been reversed.

I know of some parents who choose to discipline when it is convenient to their schedule. What a recipe for conflict. One time an action is ignored and then another time the same action brings discipline. And we wonder why our children are confused? Could this be a reason for the lack of respect for the law that permeates our society?

Take the same scenario from above and apply convenient parenting to loving and building security and self esteem in a child. Could this be a reason for the increase in adolescent suicides? Is it possible the lack of love and attention not only contributes to suicide but also to the attitude that life in general is cheap? Children are killing children, and we had better take notice and do something about it.

Parenting is not part-time nor only when it is convenient. Our children are special to God, and He desires that we take good care of them.

Bad Company

"Do not be misled: "Bad company corrupts good character." 1 Corinthians 15:33 NIV.

I don't know about you, but I sometimes take on the characteristics of the people that I am around. Regrettably, my actions and my speech sometime will change with the company I keep. In truth, this happens too many of us, but it really does not make it any more right.

When it comes to matters of character, especially good Christian character, the wrong company can become a trap. What does a Christian businessman have in common with an immoral or corrupt partner or business venture? What witness is found in a business that is based on lies or takes advantage of the fallen state of mankind?

Being somewhat of a cynic, I have often said that if you send an honest man into politics, he will become corrupt. I probably should not be saying that, but watching the news seems to give some validity to the statement. Heaven knows we could use some integrity in our politics.

As a parent I watched the company that my children kept. If I knew a person or a group of people had well-deserved dubious reputations, I did not allow my children to associate with them. If that is good for my children, then it should also be a standard for me. Does this mean absolutely no contact? Not necessarily. I would not let my child become a member of a gang, but I would not prohibit them witnessing to a gang member in a safe environment. Likewise, I do not as a businessman want to be involved with dishonest people and their transactions. But shouldn't I be prepared to give my witness for Christ to anyone who needs it?

There is a line (and it may be hard to see at times) that has been drawn and we need to know it should not be crossed. If we go too far, our character can be corrupted. That is how sin works. Watch the company you keep. If your behavior changes for the bad, you have gone too far. Don't destroy a good witness any longer. Change company. Do not be misled.

Friendship

—⁓⁓—

"Greater love has no one than this, that he
lay down his life for his friends."

John 15:13 NIV.

In our journey through this life we come across
many people. Some are just faces and have no
affect or impact on our lives. Others are people we
know and recognize, and to some extent, from a
distance, affect the way we live. Then there are those
who become what we refer to as acquaintances. We
know them fairly well and socially we have some
sort of bond. Many times we consider these people
to be friends of ours, but they are not the ones we go
to in times of trouble or triumph.

A true friend is like the one found in the verse
from the gospel of John. That person will lay down
his life for you. Not a physical death, but that can
and does happen in some extreme cases. The person
I am talking about is willing to give of his time
and resources when you need them. He will put his

interests behind your needs. This friend laughs with you and cries with you. He is with you through the good and the bad times. Often this person has a closer bond with you than your own family.

I am so thankful that I have some friends like that. Some have been with me since childhood; others are more recent friendships. Some stem from family relationships while others come about through social connections. Some hard and fast friendships got their start in grade school. Some have come through the church and Christian organizations. They are all precious, and I value them highly.

One earthly friendship stands above the rest. My wife is by far the very best friend I could have. We have been that way since high school. I would die for her and she for me. There is nothing that cannot be put on hold if one of us has a need. The greatest aspect of our friendship is we both understand that we are both serving the same God and that our friendship with Him comes before our own.

Jesus laid down His life for mankind. He wants to be our friend and be a part of our daily life. He wants to be the foundation for all friendships. The question is, "Do you want to be his friend?"

Do Good

"Command them to do good, to be rich in deeds, and to be generous and willing to share."

1 Timothy 6:18 NIV

Are you a doer of good deeds? The passage above was written to instruct people who had earthly wealth to use it for God's good purposes. Financial wealth has many times destroyed a Christian's witness. The world is full of people who have chased the dream of financial independence only to find that once it has been achieved, they have missed out on living a happy and fulfilled life.

Don't we all know people who have been so wrapped up in their careers that they neglected the people who loved them the most, only to realize the damage when it was too late? How many families have been torn apart over wealth or the drive for it? How many spouses and children have lived in neglect due to selfish ambition? How many good deeds went undone because money was more important than helping? How many friends have suffered and were not helped because it was inconvenient to someone's career track?

Someday we all will be called to account for how we used our wealth and time, whether great or small, to further God's kingdom. Personally, I want to be considered a 'do-gooder' by God's standards. Let the world scoff or make fun of me. I had rather be considered a fool by this world than to disappoint my God. Besides, when we do good deeds, don't we feel better about ourselves and others? I like feeling good, and I bet you do too.

We need to do good deeds and be willing to share with those who are in need. The best good deed we can do is to share our faith. This is not always done with words. Sometimes it takes actions. It may take money and it may take time. The question for us is, "Who is in charge of our money and our time?"

Let's all become greater doers of good deeds. We can all take more time for family and friends. We can all be more generous to those who are in need. We can all give of ourselves to those who are lost. And most importantly we can all remember who has allowed us to prosper. Thank you God for all you have given me, and may I give to others as generously as you have to me.

Damaged Goods

―――― ∞∞ ――――

"Therefore we do not lose heart. Though outwardly we are wasting away, yet inwardly we are being renewed day by day. For our light and momentary troubles are achieving for us an eternal glory that far outweighs them all." 2 Corinthians 4:16-17 NIV

Physically speaking, six surgeries, a few broken bones, dislocated fingers and now the development of arthritis in some of my joints, I am damaged goods. I am certain that most people reading this also have a list of ailments and bodily repairs. The truth is, even the great athletes have experienced physical breakdowns of some kind. Keeping this in mind, we can conclude that all of us are physically, damaged goods.

The same can be said for our spiritual beings. Worries, frustrations, heartbreaks, trials and tribulations have given us opportunity to make bad choices and sin against a holy God. Each time we have sinned, we have damaged our spirit and become damaged goods.

What do you do with your damaged possessions? Sometimes they are repairable. With the right training, one can take a broken item and make it almost as good as new. I say almost because even if you replace parts, it is never actually new again. Sometimes repairs are done through hammering, remolding or mending. Usually the result is less than perfect, leaving some of the damage noticeable. And then there are times when the damage is so severe that we have to discard that possession.

What if God took such an approach to our spiritual beings? Could you be fixed? Or would you be discarded? Well, do not get depressed. God does not work that way. Thank you, God! He does not repair us spiritually; He renews us. He makes us new again. And He does this continually for those who believe. The Scriptures tell us that it is a daily or continuous process. This wonderful process is available to everyone, but is only given to those who choose to accept it through Jesus Christ. We choose to be His and He makes us new, day in and day out.

Friend, like me, you may be damaged goods physically, but what are you spiritually? Damaged or new, God has left that choice up to you.

I Lost a Friend Today

———— ⊗⊗ ————

> "Do not forsake your friend and the friend
> of your father, and do not go to your broth-
> er's house when disaster strikes you: better a
> neighbor nearby than a brother far away."
>
> Proverbs 27:10 NIV

Today I received news that a good friend of mine lost his battle with cancer. I hugged his wife of many years and consoled her, the best I knew how. He will be missed by many friends and family members.

Harold and I had a special relationship. He raised chickens and sold their eggs. I was always ready to buy those eggs. Harold and I both agreed that eggs that came from chickens that were able to walk on the ground and scratch the good earth were better tasting than those eggs that came from the big commercial operations. We spent considerable time talking about the virtues of eggs and raising chickens. I would tease

Harold when the chickens would go on strike and not lay eggs for long periods of time.

During these periods we would talk of the virtue of fried chicken and how much better it tasted when it was not mass produced.

My friend, Harold, almost always wore a smile on his face. Even when the doctors first found cancer he remained upbeat. Our talk moved from eggs and chickens to God's grace and provision. I constantly prayed for him and it appeared for a while that maybe he would beat this awful disease. In fact, he did go into a time of remission. We both rejoiced. Later, we both cried when he was informed that new spots of cancer had been found.

We continued to talk as often as possible but never again about the eggs or chickens. We remained focused on God and how great He was and how good He had been to both of us. We talked about our relationships with our Savior and how good Heaven would be. We discussed many things but we never let our conversation become pessimistic. We spoke only of joy, hope, family and friends.

I lost a friend today. Well, not really. I will see him again in Heaven, and we will sit together at the great feast and eat the best eggs ever while we talk with Jesus.

Dedicated to my friend Harold,

David W. Thompson

Remembrance

—∞∞—

"Look to the Lord and his strength; seek his face always. Remember the wonders he has done, his miracles, and the judgments he has pronounced,"

1 Chronicles 16:11-12 NIV.

Once again I find myself admitting that I have learned a very important lesson from my wife. The other morning I took time to look at our calendar that we keep on the wall in our kitchen. In all honesty, I was just checking on what day my birthday was going to fall. My wife is very meticulous in organizing her month and if you want to know in advance what is going on in our lives for the month, this is where the information will be found.

After making sure she had not forgotten my 52nd birthday I read on; doctor's appointments, business meetings, other family member's birthdates, business conventions and then something else. Two dates suddenly stood out. The first date had my youngest son's name on it. It was his baptism anniversary. That was sixteen years ago! The next date had my oldest son's name written on it. It said "saved on this day". That was 23 years ago! I was completely amazed.

I asked my wife how long she had been doing this, and her reply was, "Ever since the day each event happened." She went on to tell me how important it was for her to remember God's blessings and to know that her boys, no matter what condition they might find themselves in, now are safe and secure in the Lord. What a testimony this was to me, as well as an awakening.

Do I take time to remember God's blessings? I do not mean just in passing. I am talking about truly memorializing these great events of my family's life and keeping them as a reminder of the Heavenly Father's provision. Life gets us so busy that many times we fail to remember what is truly important and who has supplied it. I can not think of a better way to help us appreciate our blessings than to write them on a calendar and carry them over from year to year. In time, I know my calendar will be so full of blessings that I may have to leave my birthday off.

Wordship or Worship

―――❧――――

"But the tax collector stood at a distance. He would not even look up to heaven, but beat his breast and said, 'God, have mercy on me, a sinner.'" Luke 18:13 NIV

Growing up in a small Baptist church in a small Missouri town, I heard many eloquent prayers offered up for the congregation by pastors and deacons. Rarely did I hear a prayer from someone who was not a leader in the church. So, naturally, as a young boy, I just assumed that in order to offer public prayers you must be a church leader. I also believed that you need to be able to pray in big and flowery words that pleased God. After all, as far as I knew, only God and the church leaders could fully understand such a great religious language.

I think it is possible that many people have had experiences similar to mine. It is no wonder that for many years I was too embarrassed to pray in public. I just did not feel adequate. In my travels through

73

this Christian life I have encountered many people who feel the same way. So much so that they have refused to ever pray out loud in public. What a shame that people are afraid and have been made to feel inadequate.

Now, I know it is not the words you use or the power of your speech but the condition of your worship. A simple prayer from the heart goes directly to the ears of a loving God. I wonder now if some of those eloquently-worded prayers ever made it past the ceiling of the church. I am not trying to pass judgment on those who can pray in such a fashion, but when my memory tells me that they were often, almost word for word, week after week, one does have to wonder. I think Jesus was making this point when He spoke of the Pharisee and the tax collector.

It is not about how great we are or how well we can pray. It is all about a sinner reaching out to a loving and forgiving God. Personally, I think we need to pray in such a way that those listening will not need a religious interpreter to help them understand. How are your prayers? Are they full of words? Or are they full of worship?

Holy Water?

"As they traveled along the road, they came to some water and the eunuch said, 'Look, here is water. Why shouldn't I be baptized?'" Acts 8:36 NIV

My now adult daughter relayed a story to me that happened when she was a member of our church's youth group. She and others from the group had attended a youth evangelism clinic. One day she noticed a young man on the street dressed in black and with multiple body piercings. She seized the moment and witnessed to him, and wouldn't you know it, God came through and the young man accepted Jesus Christ as his Lord and Savior. After further discussion he decided that he wanted to be baptized. With the help of a youth pastor, my daughter and others arranged to use the local swimming pool.

Another story with a happy ending, you say? No, not at all. The baptism almost did not happen. The officials of the clinic told my daughter and the youth pastor that they felt the use of the pool was inappropriate because it was not in a church. After considerable debate, they consented to the baptism, but refused to attend or acknowledge the commitment being made. I wonder what the young man, a baby in Christ, must have thought.

Where did the idea originate from that you must be baptized in a church building? And where is it written that one denomination's baptism is better than another's? I have heard church leaders insist that a person must be baptized again because the first one was performed in a church of a different denomination. What about the person who was baptized in a river? Oh, yes, that reminds me. Wasn't Jesus baptized in a river called the Jordan?

The point is that when we are baptized for the right reason, it is not into a denomination. We are acknowledging that we are aligning our life to Jesus Christ. We are becoming a member of His family. How have we strayed so far from the truth?

Now to give you a conclusion to my daughter's story. She and the youth pastor who performed the baptism in the pool were never invited back to the evangelism clinic. My daughter still rejoices in doing the right thing, and the pastor considers it one of his greatest moments. God bless them.

Time versus Opportunity

—◈◈◈—

"But Martha was distracted by all the preparations that had to be made. She came to him and asked, 'Lord, don't you care that my sister has left me to do the work by myself? Tell her to help me!' 'Martha, Martha,' the Lord answered, 'you are worried and upset about many things, but only one thing is needed. Mary has chosen what is better, and it will not be taken away from her.'"

Luke 10:40-42 NIV

Time seems to be an issue for all of us. We have become so busy that time is a commodity that we just can not get enough of. We plan out our days, weeks and months. In some cases we plan years in advance. But it never fails that we find ourselves scrambling to make deadlines and engagements.

Personally, I think this is a clever plan that the devil has devised to stop Christians from following the great commission. If he can keep us busy with a lot of little things, then we are more likely to miss the opportunities we have to witness. He conveniently has given us the excuse, "I just don't have time." It is an excuse, not the truth.

Take a moment to ponder this. If Christ had said, "I am much too busy right now. I can not make this sacrifice. They will have to wait until I have more time," where would we be? If we do not make time to take the opportunity, we may be condemning our neighbor or family member to a life without Christ.

And a life without Christ is an eternity in hell.

How much of your time is your child or grand-child worth? How about your spouse, brother, sister or parent? Are you too busy to tell your neighbor about Christ? If you do not tell them, can you be sure that someone else will?

If I can plan a day on the golf course or a family vacation, then I should be able to schedule time to talk to someone about Christ. All the plans we make in this life are temporary. You plan it. You do it. It is over. Why not reserve some time for something that will last forever? Or are you too busy?

The Passion

⸻❧⸻

"Jesus said, 'Father, forgive them for they
do not know what they are doing.'"

Luke 23:34 NIV

Much has been said about the <u>Passion of Christ</u>.
Mel Gibson's movie concerning the cruci-
fixion has caused many to stop and think about the
ultimate sacrifice that was made for us. Every year at
Easter, countless numbers of Christians will stop and
contemplate what Jesus did that day.

Jesus is our example for passion. His passion was
to love sinners and to save them from certain destruction. He was so passionate that He gave himself,
body and soul, to that cause. It is not that He suffered
so greatly, but that He did it knowing that He would
suffer, at the hands of those whom He wanted to
save. He had counted the cost and determined that
we were worth it.

Where is that passion today? It exists in those
who follow Him. Sometimes we may not show it.

In fact, there are times when we run from it. But it is always there in the believer. Some believers are called to give their life for His cause. Missionaries are martyred every day, giving their life for something greater than themselves. We all too well know that in some countries being a Christian is an offense that carries the death sentence.

Not all Christians are called to lay down their physical lives for God. But we are all called to lay down our earthly lives (our desires and passions) for His passion. We are to love the lost sinner so much that we are willing to risk our social status and prestige to bring him to Christ. This is easier said than done. I would love to tell you that you can follow my example, but to do that would be folly. I am a sinner saved by grace, who is in need of greater passion. How about you?

Let us pray. Oh loving God, grow in us the passion of your son, Jesus. We have been given the Holy Spirit. May we learn to listen to the Spirit and act on the passion that You have placed in us. Make Christ's passion our own. Amen.

First Impressions

"So whether you eat or drink or whatever you do, do it all for the glory of God. Do not cause anyone to stumble, whether Jews, Greeks or the church of God."

1 Corinthians 10:31-32 NIV.

I wonder what kind of impression I make on people the first time they meet me. For certain, there are times when I make a good impression. But just as certain, I know that at times my actions and my talk leave a less than desirable impression. In other words, I can make a bad impression just as easily as a good one.

As a Christian, I need to be on guard because I do not represent myself alone. I may only get one chance to affect a persons' life. Will it be for the good? Will they see Christ in me? Or will I be a stumbling block?

Recently, I received a letter from a new pastor in our community. It was to lodge a complaint about something that had involved customer service with the business of which I am president. He had a legitimate complaint and I handled it promptly. His tone in his letter, unfortunately, did not leave me with a very good first impression. I also was informed that his visit to one of my facilities was less than admirable. I will not judge this pastor by these actions because I know I could have easily done the same. This incident did make me stop and think about how people may view me.

Now, more than ever, it is my intention to leave a good impression wherever I may go. I want others to see something that is worthy of having. I want others to see that a personal relationship with Christ is meaningful and something to be desired. I may not always live up to my own expectations, but it will no longer be excused in my heart.

My prayer for myself and other Christians is that others will be impressed as they look past us and see the Savior of the world.

Work to Do

— ⊗⊗⊗ —

"..., his work will be shown for what it is, because the Day will bring it to light. It will be revealed with fire, and the fire will test the quality of each man's work. If what he has built survives, he will receive his reward."

1 Corinthians 3:13-14 NIV

I have good news. I woke up today! And if you are reading this article so did you. If God has chosen that we should stay here for a while longer, then we have work to do. God's work should be our most important priority. Sadly, we are not always able to say God's work is at the top of our list. God wants us to be actively working to further His Kingdom.

It is my belief, that if we would ingrain the basics of God's work into our daily lives, we would become more consistent workers. If we would study the Bible daily, we would have more knowledge. If we prayed daily, and I mean really prayed, we would have better instructions. If we took time to participate in ministries, we would gain confidence. If we serve others without grumbling about our task, we would show the humility of Christ. These basics equip us for service.

The work we accomplish for selfish gain will not stand the test of time. It may bring us earthly comfort. It may bring us fame and fortune. It will not however, bring us closer to the goal of hearing God say to us, "Well done thou good and faithful servant." The truth is, what we do here will stand or fall when our motives are judged. You can build church buildings all your life, but if it is done for earthly reasons or as a bribe to get you into Heaven, you will be greatly disappointed. Yet you can give a small glass of water to a thirsty co-worker in God's kingdom, and your reward will not be taken away.

Today and every day of your life you have a choice. Will you go to work for personal gain? Or will someone personally gain from God working through you?

How Long?

⸺〰⸻

"We sent Timothy, who is our brother and God's fellow worker in spreading the gospel of Christ, to strengthen and encourage you in your faith, so that no one would be unsettled by these trials. You know quite well that we were destined for them."

1 Thessalonians 3:2-3 NIV

Have you ever caught yourself asking, "When are my trials going to end?" Well, there is no need to feel like the lone ranger. I have asked God that question many times and almost always received the same answer. "Oh, son, it could be a lot worse." My wife and I were discussing all the trials we have experienced in just the last 10 years. The list is very lengthy. Illness, death, divorce, family quarrels and church splits are just a few. Quite honestly, it has been enough to make a person pull his hair out. Fortunately for me, I have no hair to grab.

What we are experiencing is nothing new. Mankind has faced hard times ever since our ancestors, Adam and his wife, Eve, got themselves evicted from the Garden of Eden. Each generation has and will face the challenges of living in a fallen world. Many Christians think that they should be protected from all the bad things that happen. I cannot find Scripture to back up that notion.

If you think you have it bad, I recommend you read the book of Job. If that doesn't work, you might want to study the life of Joseph. He went from privilege to slavery. He was falsely accused and put in prison. He did good deeds in prison but was forgotten. God raised him to a position of power, but he still died in a foreign country and his people were made slaves. The truth is that God's people experience hard times just like anyone else.

If there is to be a difference, it is how the Christian handles the trials he or she must walk through.

The trials we face may wear us down but they do not have to defeat us. They make us weary, but God will use them to make us stronger. Trials are like exercise. Without some pain there can be no gain.

More Juice, Please

"Since we live by the Spirit, let us keep in step with the Spirit." Galatians 5:25 NIV

My family is a major source of inspiration for my writings. This week it came from my daughter, her two sons and their dog. The dog's name is Charlie, and he was a gift from Grandpa. Charlie was obtained through an animal shelter as a puppy. He was reported to be a pure- bred Bassett hound. We now refer to him as a "who's your daddy Bassett Hound."

Charlie is now two and a half years old and if he were a person one would have to say he has ADD (Attention Deficit Disorder). Recently, the family decided that some obedience training would be of great value. The cost of doggie school being what it is, my daughter opted to purchase a shocker collar instead. In the first day of training, when Charlie tried to pull my grandson's arm out of socket and did not yield to the command to heel, the button was pushed.

We did not know that dogs could fly and neither did Charlie. Within 10 minutes, Charlie became a changed dog.

I am using this story to illustrate how God sometimes has to use the Holy Spirit to get our attention. I am sure that many of us can remember how, as new Christians, the Holy Spirit would jolt us back into reality. That sharp prick to the heart when we were pulling away from God helped us to stay close to our master. That soft compassionate voice that said, "You know better than to do that." Just like Charlie, we all could use some obedience training.

As time passes, we have a tendency to get callused to the shock administered by the trainer. We don't feel the jolt or prick as we pull on the leash of free will. We venture out of God's safety zone and find ourselves running wild on life's highway. Just like a dog playing on the highway, we risk injury and death. We can lose our potential to advance God's kingdom. Maybe we should consider asking God to turn up the dial on His training device. I would much rather get a shock than to become a shocking example. How about you?

Do it Right the First Time

⤙⤛⤜

"Whatever you do, work at it with all your heart, as working for the Lord, not for men, since you know that you will receive an inheritance from the Lord as a reward. It is the Lord Christ you are serving."

Colossians 3:23-24 NIV

I know this is hard for some men to admit. How many times have you tried to put together a toy, piece of equipment, or furniture without reading the instructions? How did that work for you? Did a half hour job turn into a two hour case of frustration? Did you have to stop partway through your project and deconstruct part of it because you forgot a part? Were there any parts left over? And the final question, did it work properly when you were done?

The independent nature of man is considered one of our best attributes, but it is also one of our worst. As we go through life we are constantly at work. Maybe not work as the world views it, but God has called us as Christians to work for His kingdom. His work does not start at 8:00 am and stop at 5:00 pm. Every second, every minute of our life is meant to be for His service.

God, being merciful and complete in understanding, knew we would need directions. He was wise enough to give us illustrations also. The Bible is available to us to guide us through life. His Son, Jesus, is the perfect illustration of Godly service and a sinless life. His teaching and that of the apostles are designed to bring our service to a perfect conclusion.

In this life we are given opportunities. We can do things right the first time if we follow Christ's example and God's word, or we can botch the job by forgetting to follow the instructions. God wants us to lead others to Him. How we lead our life and treat others will have a lasting impression. If we do not follow the directions, we are delivering less than the best. Also, we may prevent the next generation from being as useful as they could be. God likes to have fully functional servants with no parts left over.

Worry? Who me?

⸺⚬⚬⚬⸺

"Therefore do not worry about tomorrow, for tomorrow will worry about itself. Each day has enough trouble of its own."

Matthew 6:34 NIV.

What are you worried about? Yes, you. We all have worries. We can put on our best faces and say, "No, I don't worry about things," but it really would not be true. I admit that some people do a better job in keeping their wits about them in times of trouble, and, therefore, seem to be worry free. The reality is we all worry, some of us more than others.

Today's busy schedules, family and economic pressures can and do cause us to worry. Finances, health, work and school are important aspects of life. When any one of them is not going well, worry is at the door. Take two or three of them malfunctioning at the same time, and you find yourself overwhelmed. At this point, if your health has not been affected it soon will be. No one will deny that excessive worry can lead to severe health problems.

Why do we worry? God promises to take care of our needs. In fact, the Bible tells us that God knows our every need. It seems to be a part of our human nature. No one likes to be in a situation that they cannot control. Some situations we can control if we do not let our worries consume us. If we can just remember that God is watching and only wants to prosper us, we can keep a clear focus on the situation at hand. When our focus is clear, worries become challenges, and challenges can be overcome. Of course, our biggest challenge is not to worry.

Life isn't easy. God never promised that it would be. He did promise that He would never leave or forsake us. God is with his children always. So what is there to worry about? The truth is-not a thing. But I am sure I will still worry from time to time. Sometimes I worry that I have a sign on my back that reads, "Work in Progress."

I Expect Service

⸺⸺

"But I tell you that men will have to give account on the Day of Judgment for every careless word they have spoken. For by your words you will be acquitted, and by your words you will be condemned."

Matthew 12:36-37

When we go to a restaurant we expect a few things. Good food, cleanliness, and most of all, friendly and prompt service. We will overlook some dirt on the floor or food not prepared exactly to our taste if the service is good. But poor service dulls our enthusiasm no matter how great the food or how wonderful the atmosphere. There is something about quality service that brings us back time and time again.

The one major problem I see with our society today is that we expect service but are not always willing to give it. I have witnessed unbelievable rudeness from people who felt they did not get the service that they deserved. Sadly, I have seen such displays come from Christians as well as non-believing people. Does poor service give us the right to be rude? My answer, and I believe God's, is no. Truth is, rudeness is not a right. It is a sin. Rudeness is the product of a selfish attitude.

Mankind wants to be served. Read your Bible and look at history. You will see the creation asking the Creator for service. You can find it in our prayers and some religious teachings. Nowhere do I find God being referred to as a waiter. We are His servants, not the other way around. We were created to serve, not to be served. Through service, we are to show the lost the way to find God. A rude attitude will send them away, not bring them back.

If you receive poor service at a restaurant, the ultimate solution is to not go back. If the non-believer is subjected to a rude Christian, his choice may be to not come back. Who ultimately answers for such a decision? The Bible says we do.

I Want More

———— ⸺ ————

"Then he said to them, 'Watch out! Be on
your guard against all kinds of greed; a man's
life does not consist in the abundance of his
possessions.'" Luke 12:15 NIV

Contrary to popular opinion, more is not always
better. We are taught that to be a success in
today's society we must accomplish more and possess
more. We need to work harder and longer to achieve
greatness. The world may judge you by your success
and accumulated wealth, but God has different and
better standards.

If wealth and possessions are so wonderful, why
do so many rich people seem to be unhappy and
unsatisfied? Why does the pursuit of riches usually
end up in the pursuit of more riches? These are very
interesting questions.

Mankind has always been in a search of perfect
happiness and contentment. Unfortunately, for the
most part, we have been looking to and for the wrong

things to fulfill these feelings. Can having ample financial resources and possessions make us happy and content? Well, of course it can. But it will only be temporary if God is not in the center of your life.

God has a plan to meet our needs, but not all our wants. As a parent, I know that what children want and what they may need are as far as the East is from the West. I also know that just because I want it, does not mean that it is good for me. In fact, the prisons are full of people who wanted something that they did not need. Need and greed may rhyme but they have nothing in common.

I cannot buy my way into Heaven. And it is from Heaven that all blessings and true happiness flow. The price for Heaven has already been paid. Not by you or me, but by Jesus Christ. My happiness comes from accepting Him as my Lord and Savior and being content with the fact that He is storing up treasures for me. Now, that is rich.

Give or Take

———❧———

"Give, and it will be given to you. A good measure, pressed down, shaken together and running over, will be poured into your lap. For with the measure you use, it will be measured to you." Luke 6:38 NIV.

I have heard this verse used many times from the pulpit to instill a financial-giving mindset. Interestingly enough, it comes from a passage that deals with judging, not tithing. Do I think that it can certainly apply to the faithful giver? Absolutely, but I also think it is very foolish to limit the scope of these profound words.

Giving goes far beyond finances. It is found in all relationships. The marriage relationship will stand or fall on the ability of two people to give to one another. If one gives and the other does nothing but take, the relationship will fail. If both parties are takers, it will be all out war. If husband and wife both give more to the relationship than they take, an amazing peace will reign in that home.

The same principles are found in the parent- child relationship. The parent who constantly gives to the child and never receives gratitude, love or respect will ultimately wear down and live in confusion. The child who gives nothing back will look for other relationships to pirate once he has depleted the parent's resources. This cycle will continue until people learn that to get the best they must give the best.

The same thing shows up at work. Your relationship with your boss or supervisor is governed by the attitude, attention and skills you give to the job. If you are just putting in your time, do not expect praise or reward. If you go the extra mile and bring enthusiasm to the work place, there is a good chance that someone will notice. Even if the boss does not, God will.

For us the biggest question is. How much are we giving to our relationships with God? Despite popular opinion, the Creator of the universe is not Santa Claus. For many people God is only there to give what they want to take. I believe it is true you cannot outgive God. But, I also believe that God has the perfect right to stop giving and blessing an ungrateful Christian.

If you want to be blessed by God, try giving to Him more than you take from Him. Personally, I think you will find the more you give, the more you will be given. You will not need to take anything. If you want better relationships, try giving more of yourself to them. After all, God gave His only Son to save a lost and dying world.

Child Abuse

"Fathers, do not embitter your children,
or they will become discouraged."
Colossians 3:21 NIV.

Few, if any people, will deny that child abuse in
our country is a very serious problem. However,
many people, including Christians, fail to see the full
implications of this social tragedy. Some people see
this as an issue of physical and sexual abuse only.
What about the child who is never told he is loved
or given a hug and a kiss? And what about the child
who is verbally abused? These are children of abuse
that many times fall between the cracks.

To never have been shown love physically or
verbally will create bitterness in a child. This bitterness will be carried throughout his life and will most
assuredly be passed on to the next generation. Do you
remember the warning found in the fourth commandment? "I, the Lord am a jealous God, punishing the
children for the sin of the fathers to the third and

fourth generation of those who hate me." This verse concerns the making of idols and the worshipping of them. I believe all child abuse comes from the idol of self-centeredness.

If you have been abused as a child, God wants to help you break the cycle. He wants you to be free from the pain. God wants you to know that you have worth. In fact, you are worth the sacrifice of His Son, Jesus Christ. You are someone who is special to God.

It is time to change the way we think. Child abuse must stop! And Christians, it must stop first in our own homes. There is no need to tell the other man how to clean his house if yours is filthy. How are you treating your children? Do you show them love? Do you give hugs and kisses on a regular basis? Are you able to correct them without becoming physically or verbally abusive? Do you give praise when it is due? We can change the world one family at a time and it starts with our own. If there is a problem with abuse in your home, God will help you make a change. The first step is found in the words of our Lord, "Go and sin no more."

What Do You Think About?

⸺ ⟨⟩ ⸺

"Finally, brothers, whatever is true, whatever is noble, whatever is right, whatever is pure, whatever is lovely, whatever is admirable – if anything is excellent or praiseworthy – think about such things."

Philippians 4:8 NIV

What in the world are you thinking about? This is a question that I ask myself all too often. Whatever you focus your mind on has a profound effect on your life. Negative thinking makes for negative people. Obsessive thinking will lead to obsessive behavior. It is well known that most child molesters and rapists have poisoned their thinking with pornography. Violent thinking more than likely will lead to violent behavior. The list can go on and on.

Fortunately, there is a better way. Imagine the difference in your life and the lives of others if we all practiced the verse above. If our thinking process was focused on the good and noble things there would be less dishonesty and corruption. If we think positively, then we are more apt to handle a crisis when it happens, rather than becoming overwhelmed and depressed. If our thoughts are pure, the family would be the safe haven God intended it to be. If our minds were filled with praise, we would be less critical of people and be better citizens in our communities. And this list can go on and on, too.

So friend, where is your mind right now? Have you been having trouble in this area? I suggest you first repent of wrong thinking and start doing something about it. A great way to start is to read the Bible daily. God has so much good He wants to show you and even more grace He wants to extend to you. He can help you change your thinking. If you change your thinking, you will change your life.

Reconciliation to God

⸻

"But God demonstrates his own love for us in this: While we were still sinners, Christ died for us. Since we have now been justified by his blood, how much more shall we be saved from God's wrath through him! For if, when we were God's enemies, we were reconciled to him through the death of his Son, how much more, having been reconciled, shall we be saved through his life! Not only is this so, but we also rejoice in God through our Lord Jesus Christ, through whom we have now received reconciliation."

Romans 5:8-11 NIV

The definition of reconcile is: to make friends again; to win over; to settle or satisfy; to bring into harmony or agreement. This process is called reconciliation. I believe that full and complete reconciliation is achieved only when we are reconciled to God, ourselves and to others.

Being reconciled to God is the first and most important step. Without this aspect, there is no base on which to build. Christ reconciled us to God. It is nothing that we have done. We cannot be in harmony with God without the redeeming work of Christ. Without accepting Christ for who He is and what He has accomplished, we will remain separated from God. Without a working relationship with God, we cannot be fully complete. We are unable to be truly reconciled to ourselves or to others without God.

As a result of our reconciliation, we have been given the ministry of reconciliation to the lost. We have become ambassadors for Christ. It is our duty to implore others on Christ's behalf to become reconciled to God. We need to be able to ask these questions. Where are you today? Are you reconciled to God through Jesus Christ? And we need to be able to give the lost the answer. Dear friend, you cannot ask someone the question unless you are able to give the answer. So, where are you today?

Once people are reconciled to God, then, and only then, are we able to begin reconciling our own lives.

Reconciled to Self

⸻

> "What is written in the Law?" he replied.
> "How do you read it?" "Love the Lord your
> God with all your heart and with all your soul
> and with all your strength and with all your
> mind; and Love your neighbor as yourself."
> "You have answered correctly," Jesus replied.
> "Do this and you will live."
>
> Luke 10:26-28 NIV

If you are not reconciled with yourself, then you cannot truly love yourself. If you do not love yourself, then your neighbor is in a lot of trouble. Why do we seem to have so many people struggling with self esteem? One answer that must be considered is that many of us have not become reconciled with ourselves.

This world works overtime to tell us that we are not good enough, young enough, smart enough, thin enough, rich enough and so on. Too often, we set our eyes on things that are not of God. My question for you is, "Who made you and me?" The answer, "God did." Do you really believe that the God of all creation makes mistakes? The Bible tells us He has numbered every hair on our head. In my case there are fewer to count, but that is not a big deal.

God does not prize one person over the other. He does allow us to go in our own separate directions in life. How we travel through life has a lasting effect, not only on ourselves, but also on others around us. If I have asked God to forgive me for something I have done, then why shouldn't I forgive myself? God has forgiven me. Am I better than God? We have a tendency to spiritually beat ourselves up even after God has erased our transgressions. We do not think we should be happy or satisfied with whom we are.

I want to live, and I want to live abundantly. I want to be happy with whom God made me to be. Who am I? The answer is really very simple. I am a sinner saved by grace, who wants to do what is right, but one who does not always do the right thing. I am made by God for His purposes, and I have a purpose. God loves me and He does not make junk.

People to People Reconciliation

⸺◦∞◦⸺

"Therefore, if you are offering your gift at the altar and there remember that your brother has something against you; leave your gift there in front of the altar. First go and be reconciled to your brother; then come and offer your gift." Matthew 5:23-24 NIV

"If your brother sins against you go and show him his fault, just between the two of you. If he listens to you, you have won your brother over." Matthew 18:15 NIV

I purposely used two passages for today's lesson. My reasoning is this. God does not allow us the option of not trying to reconcile our differences. The first verse tells me if I know that I have wronged my brother, I need to go and make amends for my actions and seek his forgiveness. The second verse tells me that if my brother has wronged me, I need not wait for him to come to me but should go to him and point out the wrong and attempt to restore our relationship.

Families and churches are being torn apart because people refuse to reconcile their differences with one another. Some of the problems are serious while others are small and petty. But, I cannot find in God's Word any reason that reconciliation of relationships should not be attempted.

I know of families that are torn apart because of real and imagined transgressions. Parents do not talk to their children and hold anger inside. Children break off their relationships with their parents over misunderstandings. Siblings refuse to see each other for years over reasons they cannot even remember. God cannot be pleased.

Truthfully, there may be reasons why a relationship can no longer be close. But as children of God, we are called to make every attempt to restore broken relationships. If we let our feelings rule us, pride will stop us from reconciling our differences with others. A life without personal reconciliations is a lonely road to travel and one I hope none of us is willing to accept.

Remember, to be truly whole, one must be reconciled to God, themselves and to others.

The Spring of Life

———— ⦶⦶⦶ ————

"Jesus answered, 'Everyone who drinks this water will be thirsty again, but whoever drinks the water I give him will never thirst, Indeed, the water I give him will become in him a spring of water welling up to eternal life.'" John 4:13-14 NIV

At the time of this writing, I am sitting in the great room of a small but wonderful lodge nestled between the giant pines of the great Rocky Mountains. The Rocky Mountain Lodge is located in Cascade, Colorado, just 19 miles from the pinnacle of Pike's Peak. Just down the highway, and I do mean down, is the city of Manitou. This city became famous in the 1800's for its many springs. These springs were reported to have healing properties, especially in the treatment of tuberculosis. The rich, famous and the poor alike traveled to this area to take the cure.

Today, people are looking for other cures. They seek cures for old and new diseases. They search for cures for emotional and spiritual diseases. They desperately hunt for the cures for their marriage and relationship problems. Many look to Hollywood icons for answers. Others think that there is a pill out there that will cure everything. Some search for solutions in the stars and through crystals. There are many places to look, but none of them are a complete guarantee, except one.

For me, there is only one true cure, and it comes from the spring of living water that can only be found in Jesus Christ. I have witnessed the living water He gives cure the deadliest cancers when modern medicine had failed. I have seen the blind and the lame made whole. I know of souls delivered from drug and alcohol addictions. I have been present when marriages and families have been restored. Many times I have watched as the Holy Spirit brought joy and peace to a troubled human spirit.

I do not shun the cures of modern medicine. I know that God has given wisdom to our doctors and scientists. But, nothing created by man can bring me eternal life in Heaven. Only the living water of God, through Jesus Christ, can cure the sinful heart of a man and restore him to God. And this, of course, is the ultimate cure.

A Personal Confession

"Do not let your hearts be troubled, Trust in God; trust also in me." John 14:1 NIV

Let me prove to you that I am human. Some time ago, a friend and a pastor of mine moved to another state. Our church was going through hard and troubling times. He had told me the he had felt God's calling and, therefore, needed to move on. I was very saddened and hurt by his leaving. But to be honest, I also felt abandoned. I thought he had surely taken the easy way out and had left me and a few others to pick up the pieces of our hurting congregation.

After three years of separation, I was able to go and visit my friend in his new location. Little did I know that God was about to show me that I had completely misjudged him. As we walked together and talked of the work he was doing in his new ministry field, conviction stabbed me in my heart. I suddenly realized that I had never forgiven my friend for leaving me. I also understood that God had truly relocated him, and that he was being used in a mighty way to reach the lost. In other words, he was exactly where God wanted him to be.

My friend never knew how I truly felt, but God certainly did. He (God) woke me up around 2:00 am and showed me my error. He showed me that what I had felt was nothing but a lie. The lie was not hurting my friend or preventing him from doing God's work. But, it was indeed a stumbling block for me. I thanked my God for the revelation and confessed my sin. What a wonderful release!

God has shown me and now I tell you, that unresolved hurts, whether real or imagined, have no place in the Christian's heart. The unresolved may be forgotten for a time but it never goes away. Is there anything unresolved in your life? Ask God to show you the truth and then resolve it once and forever. Trust in Him.

Where is your Quiet Place?

"Then, because so many people were coming and going that they did not even have a chance to eat, he said to them, 'Come with me by yourselves to a quiet place and get some rest.'" Mark 6:31 NIV

Where do you go to be alone with the Lord? Where do you find rest for your weary soul? It may be on a mountain top such as I have seen in Colorado. It may be in the peace and solitude of a garden or forest. Maybe your quiet place is in a chapel or just a quiet cozy room. Wherever it may be, remember the most important part is going with Jesus.

"Come with me by yourselves to a quiet place and get some rest." Take these words to heart. Too many Christians push themselves until they are so tired that they are unable to serve. Sometimes we call it burnout. God does not ask us to burn out, but to serve

Him to the best of our ability. We are more capable in our service when we are rested and restored.

God does not want us to be Energizer bunny Christians. Our physical, mental and spiritual batteries do and will run down. It is important that we take the time that is necessary to recharge and refresh. Find your place of rest and recharging. Go there from time to time. I know that God will be waiting for you. He desires more than just your service. He wants to have some one-on-one personal time. He wants to have a relationship with you that is personal, not just a master/servant one.

Hey friend, the Bible tells us that even Jesus became weary and needed rest. John 4:6 tells us this, "Jacob's well was there, and Jesus, tired as He was from the journey, sat down by the well. It was about the sixth hour." I know that my strength and capacity for work is no match for the Son of God, and I hope you understand that also. God wants you and me to burn bright, not burn out.

The Perfect Child

⟨⟩

"Train a child in the way he should go,
and when he is old he will not turn from it."
Proverbs 22:6 NIV

This one is for every Christian parent who thinks they have failed God by not raising the perfect child. If your child is not perfect, do not despair or think yourself a failed parent. The truth is that no one can parent without disappointment and failure.

As a Christian, you know you are a child of God. So, let me ask you this question. Did you become His child because you were perfect? If you were perfect, then you would not need Jesus Christ as your Savior. If you and I are not perfect, how can we teach or create another to be perfect?

The Bible teaches us that all have sinned. Does that mean that God, who created you and me, is a bad parent? I say, not at all. Doesn't God teach us through His perfect Word? Don't we have the Holy Spirit to guide us through our daily journeys? Didn't

Jesus have to pay our ransom at Calvary? And yet, we still do not live perfect lives.

Dear parent, never stop trusting in God's word. Never stop teaching your child, no matter what age, God's truth. Continue to pray for the Holy Spirit to move in your child's life. Remember, your child is only human and was born imperfect. They will make choices that we will not like. Many times they make the very same choices we did ourselves. It is only because we have suffered the consequences that we now know they were bad ones.

We can never raise perfect children, but we can give them our love and tell them of God's love. We can train from our mistakes. Be honest with them. Help them to understand that Jesus died for them also. Train them in the way they should go by leading them to Jesus who said, "I am the way."

The Color of the Day

—❦—

"But our citizenship is in heaven. And we eagerly await a Savior from there, the Lord Jesus Christ, who, by the power that enables him to bring everything under his control, will transform our lowly bodies so that they will be like his glorious body."

Philippians 3:20-21 NIV

It is late October now, and as I travel around the area, the trees are awash with color. Shades of greens, yellows, oranges and reds cover the hills as well as our city streets. It is a beautiful sight to behold. The changing of the colors serves to remind me that life is always in a state of change.

Very soon the colors will fade and there will be more browns than anything else. Most of the leaves will fall from the trees that had given them life and color. They will be a crunchy reminder of what had once been as I walk through the forest. Isn't that how life works? One day life is green and you are full of health and vitality. Before you know it, life happens, and you sense a change in the air.

Youth and optimism wanes as bad things happen to good people. People you have grown to trust and admire begin to disappoint you, or worse, betray your trust. Your green days become fewer and the colors that come from living in a lost world begin to show.

Relationships come and go. Each one has a lasting effect on our color. Health issues may drain some or all of our physical energy, leaving our outward appearance less than what we would have hoped for. Stress from work will often alter our shade. After ten or twenty years in the same job situation, life may dull our green or even turn us to a dull yellow or a burning red.

Life gives us color. Life makes us who we are. In this world we do not have the ability to stay evergreen. Our bodies change and everything around us changes also. It is just a part of it. Not all changes are bad. God rewards us with the coloring of marriage and parenthood. He brightens us with spiritual and personal victories. He deepens us through love. And He sustains us with his grace.

One day when all our color is gone and our branches have fallen, God will call us home. He will then make us a new body. This one will be evergreen and it will be constantly nourished by the very presence of God Almighty.

Printed in the United States
201622BV00002B/115-231/P

9 781604 774719